A Pictorial Souvenir of Exotic
Cornish Gardens

Photography by Derek Harris

First Published in 2002
by
The WoodLand & Garden Publishing Company,
34 Nene Valley Business Park, Oundle, Peterborough, Cambs, PE8 4HN

Photography Copyright Derek Harris

ISBN 1 899803 17 3

Designed by The WoodLand & Garden Publishing Company

Pictures used in this book, other photographic work and prints by Derek Harris are available from
The WoodLand & Garden Picture Library
34 Nene Valley Business Park, Oundle, Peterborough, Cambs, PE8 4HN.
Tel: 01832 270077   Fax: 01832 270088
Email: derekharris.associates@virgin.net

Cover picture: Treve Holman Memorial Bridge, Chyverton Garden

Introduction

Bounded on either flank by the warm waters of the Gulf Stream the narrow, rugged peninsular which is Cornwall contains the greatest collection of famous exotic gardens in the world.

For over 200 years plant collectors have sent newly discovered seed and plant material from every continent to be raised by the skilled and dedicated Cornish gardeners. Visitors to Cornwall today will find and wonder at the vibrant colour and scent of the huge mature specimens of trees and shrubs which would take a lifetime of travel to find in their native habitat.

This small souvenir takes a journey from the exciting new millennium Eden Project in the East to Pine Lodge, The Lost Gardens of Heligan, Caerhays, Trewithen, Chyverton and on to the stunning gardens of Trebah and The Abbey Gardens on Tresco, Isles of Scilly in the far West.

Tony Hibbert
Trebah

The Eden Project

Humid Tropics Biome
Bodelva, St Austell
Cornwall PL24 2SG
Tel: 01726 811911

5. Shimenawa of rice straw rope commonly used in Japanese sacred Shinto areas

6. Entering the Biome

7. Travellers Palm

8. Deep in the Biome

9. Oceanic Islands

10. Waterfall

11. A theatrical spice boat

12. Story telling

13. Rock painting by Francisco Montes Shunna

14. Rock painting by Yolanda Panduro

15. *Heliconia*

17. *Guzmania*

16. *Vriesea*

18. Pineapple and *Codiaeum variegatum*

19. *Calliandra haematocephala*

21. *Hymenocallis caribaea*

20. *Begonia pseudo*

22. *Anthurium* 'Flamingo Flower'

Pine Lodge Gardens

Holmbush
St Austell
Cornwall PL25 3RQ
Tel: 01726 73500

23. *Rhododendron sinogrande*

24. Japanese Garden

25. Cornus alba and camellias by the pond

26. Grasses in the Slave Garden

27. *Clematis armandii* 'Apple Blossom'

28. *Acacia pravissima*

29. Japanese Garden

30. Puma

31. Engine House

32. View from the Japanese Garden

Lost Gardens of Heligan

Pentewan
St Austell
Cornwall PL26 6EN
Tel: 01726 845100

33. Agave

34. The Jungle at the Lost Gardens of Heligan

35. Group of Tree Ferns *Dicksonia antarctica* in The Jungle

36. Magnificent *Rhododendron* 'Cornish Red' in The Jungle

37. Deep in The Jungle

38. Skunk Cabbage *Lysichiton americanus*

39. Vegetables on parade

40. Sweet William in the Vegetable Garden

41. The Melon Garden

42. The Sundial Garden

43. The Italian Garden

44. The Italian Garden

Caerhays Castle Garden

Gorran
St Austell
Cornwall PL26 6LY
Tel: 01872 501310

45. *Magnolia* 'Caerhays Surprise'

46. Caerhays Castle

47. A fine example of *Michelia doltsopa* in full flower

48. *Michelia doltsopa* flowers

49. Spring selection of primulas and cyclamen

50. Kaleidoscope of spring colours

51. Rhododendrons and Azaleas on the Main Ride

52. *Pieris* 'Forest Flame' with primroses

53. Spring carpet of primroses

54. Magnolias, rhododendrons and camellias on the Main Ride

Trewithen Gardens

Truro
Cornwall
TR2 4DD
Tel: 01726 883647

55. *Ceanothus arboreus* 'Trewithen Blue'

56. The Main Lawn to the house

57. Colourful panorama of Rhododendrons and Azaleas

58. Rhododendrons and Azaleas

59. Pieris and Azaleas

60. Spring flowers in The Cockpit

61. *Clianthus puniceus*

62. *Hydrangea paniculata*

Chyverton

Zelah
Truro
Cornwall TR4 9HD
Tel: 01872 540324

63. Spring view to the house

64. Treve Holman Memorial Bridge

65. The lakeside in early spring

66. Spring colour on the Main Drive

67. Evening sunshine by the Treve Holman Bridge

68. Hybrid orchids by the bridge

69. Bridge with stream full of *Lysichiton americanus*

70. Azalea by lichen covered seat

71. Azaleas and bluebells by lichen covered seat

72. *Acer palmatum* 'Atropurpureum'

Trebah

Mawnan Smith
Falmouth
Cornwall TR11 5JZ
Tel: 01326 250448

73. Chusan Palms *Trachycarpus fortunei*

74. View of the house from Petry's Path

75. Misty morning with *Rhododendron* 'Cornish Red'

76. Rhododendron Valley

77. Tree Ferns *Dicksonia antarcctica* below the Zig-Zag

78. *Agapanthus* with Tree Ferns on the Zig-Zag

79. Colourful Water Garden in late spring

80. Koi Pool with carp and Tree Ferns

81. *Zantiedeschia aethiopica* with Candelabra Primulas

82. *Zantiedeschia aethiopica* with Candelabra Primulas

83. Iris's and Candelabra Primulas

84. Candelabra Primulas and Iris's

85. Bluebells beneath a Beech tree

86. Azaleas by copper beech

87. Hydrangea Valley

88. Rhododendron Valley

Tresco Abbey Garden

Tresco
Isles of Scilly
TR24 0QQ
Tel: 01720 424105

89. *Aloe arborescens*

90. The Middle Terrace showing a selection of what is so unique and special to the Abbey Gardens

91. *Furcraea longaeva* and Neptune's Steps

92. *Echium callithyrsum* on the Middle Terrace

93. The East Rockery

94. *Furcraea* and agave in the East Rockery

95. The Old Abbey ruins with *Aeoniums*

96. Wall plugged with brightly coloured *Lampranthus*

97. *Echium callithyrsum* in a mixed border

98. Pergola on the Middle Terrace

99. *Protea cynaroides* 'King Protea'

101. *Fascicularia bromeliaceae*

100. *Scilla peruriana*

102. *Aeonium*